A-Z STAINES and CHERTSEY

CONTENTS

REFERENCE

Motorway	**M3**	Airport	✈	
A Road	**A308**	Car Park (selected)	Ⓟ	
B Road	**B376**	Church or Chapel	†	
Dual Carriageway		Fire Station	■	
One-way Street		Hospital	Ⓗ	
Traffic flow on A roads is indicated by a heavy line on the driver's left.	→	House Numbers (A & B Roads only)	13	8
Junction Name	APEX CORNER	Information Centre	🅸	
Restricted Access		National Grid Reference	510	
Pedestrianized Road		Police Station	▲	
Track & Footpath		Post Office	★	
Residential Walkway		Toilet:		
Railway	Tunnel / Level Crossing	without facilities for the Disabled	▽	
		with facilities for the Disabled	▽	
Stations:		Disabled facilities only	▽	
National Rail Network	⮀	Educational Establishment	◰	
Underground	●	Hospital or Hospice	◰	
Built-up Area	PARK / AV	Industrial Building	◰	
Local Authority Boundary	— ∙ — ∙ —	Leisure or Recreational Facility	◰	
Posttown Boundary		Place of Interest	◰	
Postcode Boundary (within posttown)		Public Building	◰	
		Shopping Centre or Market	◰	
Map Continuation	▲ 12	Other Selected Buildings	◰	

SCALE

1:15,840	0	¼	½	¾ Mile
4 inches to 1 mile	0	250 500 750		1 Kilometre

6.31 cm to 1 km
10.16 cm to 1 mile

Copyright of Geographers' A-Z Map Company Limited

Fairfield Road, Borough Green, Sevenoaks, Kent TN15 8PP
Telephone: 01732 781000 (Enquiries & Trade Sales)
01732 783422 (Retail Sales)

www.a-zmaps.co.uk

Ordnance Survey This product includes mapping data licensed from Ordnance Survey® with the permission of the Controller of Her Majesty's Stationery Office.

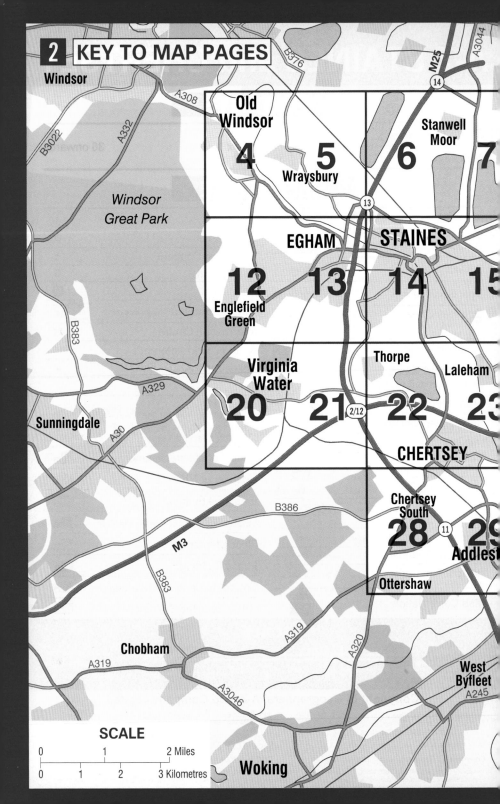

Windsor

Old Windsor

4

5
Wraysbury

Stanwell Moor

6

7

A308

A332

B3022

A332

A3044

M25

14

Windsor Great Park

B383

A329

Sunningdale

A30

B383

M3

EGHAM

12
Englefield Green

13

STAINES

14

15

13

Virginia Water

20

21
2/12

Thorpe

22

Laleham

23

CHERTSEY

B386

Chertsey South

28

11

29
Addlest

Ottershaw

Chobham

A319

A319

A3046

A319

A320

West Byfleet

A245

SCALE

0   1   2 Miles

0   1   2   3 Kilometres

Woking

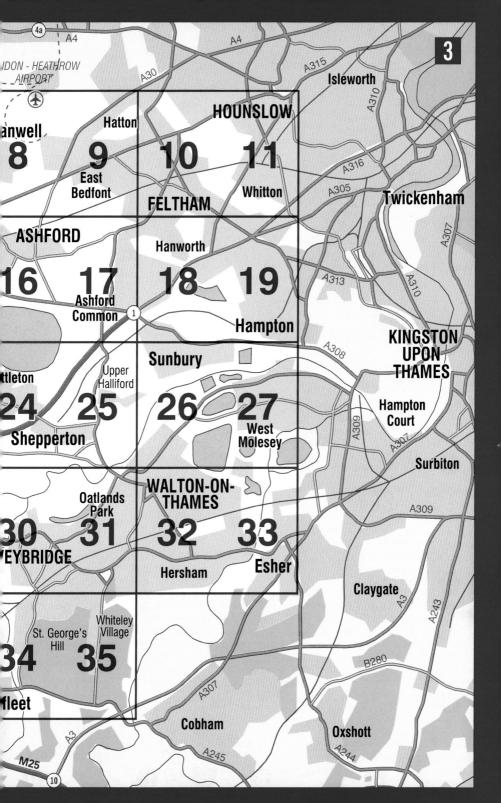

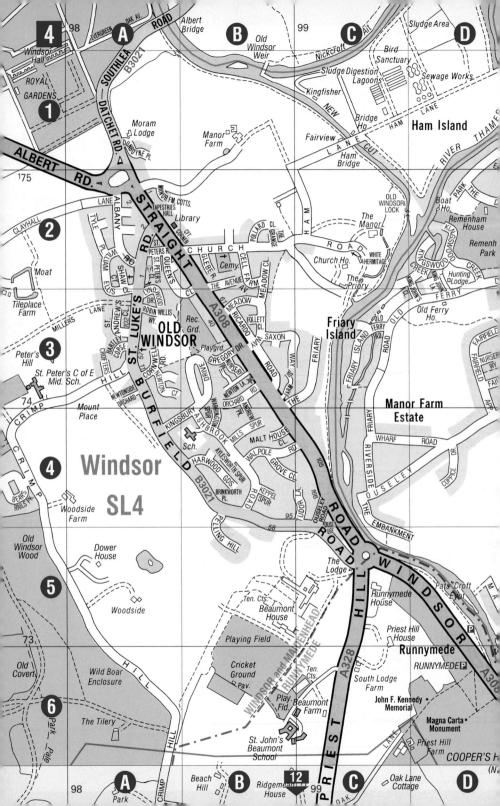

Nurseries

WESTERN

ROAD

Airside   Road   Tunnel

R. Colne

Works

BEDFONT
COURT
ESTATE

SPOUT LANE N.

BEDFONT

**Hounslow
TW6**

1

PORT   A3113

STANWELL

A3044

PERIMETER

The Mill

175

FLINTLOCK
CL.

SPOUT

LANE

MERVIA
VINE CL.

SOUTHERN COTTS.

SHELL CL.
BANK CL.

IGLEW'N DR.

HORTON

WAY

ROAD

SANDRINGHAM RD.

2

SOUTHERN

ROAD

HILLINGDON   PERIMETER

SPELTHORNE

RIVER
SIDE

RIVERSIDE RD.

ROAD

Recreation
Ground

Playgrd.

Gravel Pit

LOWLANDS
DR.

HENDON
WY.

LIN

DAY CL.

STANWELL

E

PERIMETER

ROAD

STANWELL
MOOR

Nurseries

ROAD

Southern
Fm.

RUSSELL
DR.

GLEB

GLENEAGLES
CL.

GLEBE
CL.

THE
STANWELL

Rec.
Grd.

UNIT

WOOD
IM.

RAVLND

WESTLAND
CL.

SEX

CLIFTON
CT.

WHITLE

3

AWS

mping   LANE

HORTON RD.

PARK

GIBSON PL.

ROBERTS

B378

CROFTERS
CL.

STAN-
HOPE

WY.
HEATH
CL.

ATHERTON
CL.

SS
WOOD

HIGH
OAKS

HOPE

ROAD

TOWN
LANE

PINE

CHRIST
CHURCH

Sch.

DOUGLAS
RD.

BRISTOL
CT.

FALCON

DR.

74

ROAD

A

Lord Knyvett
CL.

STANWELL

8

DUTCH
BARN CL.

APP.

TRINITY

HADFIELD

EVEREST
RD.

COMET RD.

WELLINGTON
RD.

CORD

Rec.
Grd.

ST. MARY'S CR.

ST. MARY'S

WEBSTER

JUBILE
CL.

MAISIE
WY.

TWN FM.
WY.

BEECH
CL.

ST. ANNE'S

HADRIAN
WY.

BRITANNIA

AIR CL.

ANDOVER

Prim.
Sch.

Lib.

FRO

CAMBRI
GDS.

4

Cemetery

JORDANS
CL.

EVERGREEN
CT.

DIAMEDES
CT.

FOXGLV

AV

VIBIA

ELIZABETHAN WAY

HADRIAN
WAY

VISCOUNT RD.

Play
Fld.

DOVE
CT.

HERON
CT.

CRANFORD CL.

CANOPUS
CL.

EXPL

STAINES

GEORGE VI

A3044

BETHAM
CL.

ENSIGN
WY.

ENSIGN

MULBERRY

CT.

B378

CLYDE

Lancaster

5

KINGSWY

ERVOIR

RESERVOIRS
(BIRD SANCTUARY)

KINGSWAY

SCOTS CL.

VIOLA

73 AV

AVENUE

HOLY

Supersto

ASHFOR
HOSP.

H

VIOLA

ENSING

6

STANWELL

ROAD

A30

LONDON

AVONDALE RD.

ROAD

ASHFOR

06

SEAT

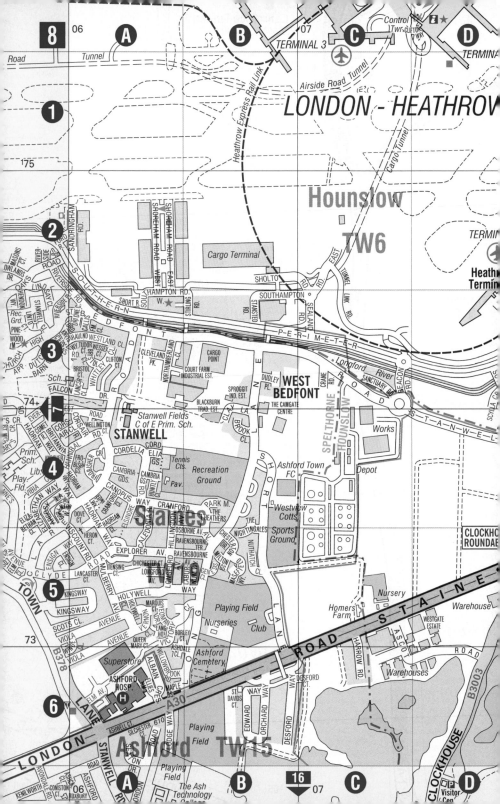

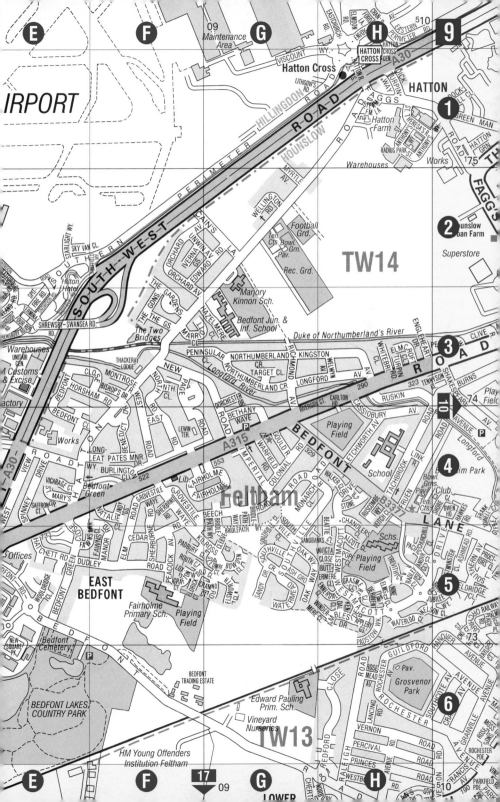

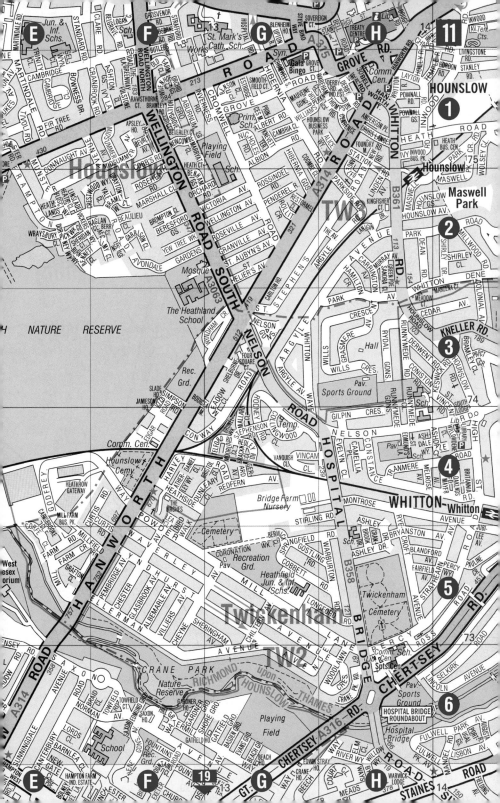

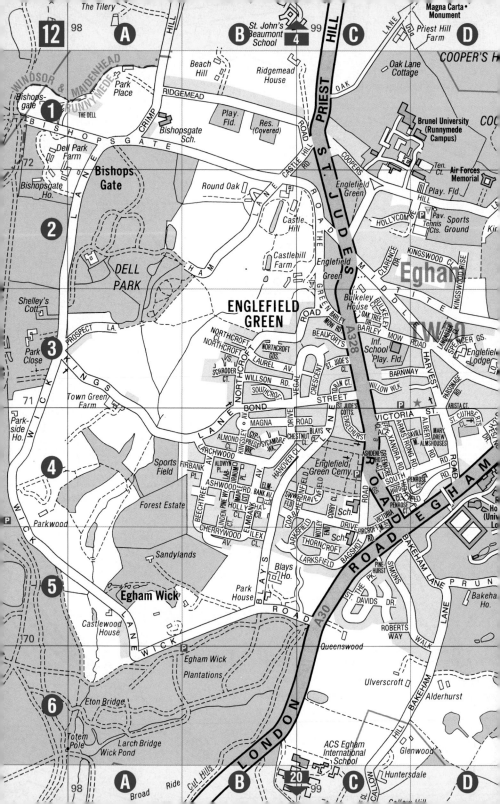

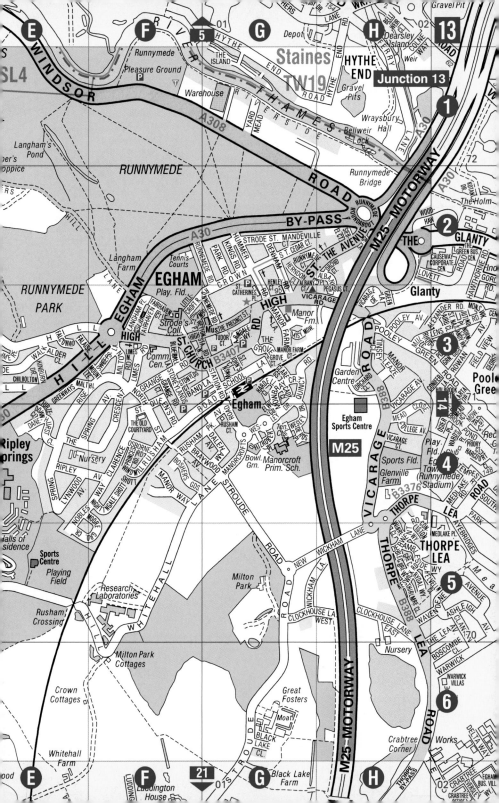

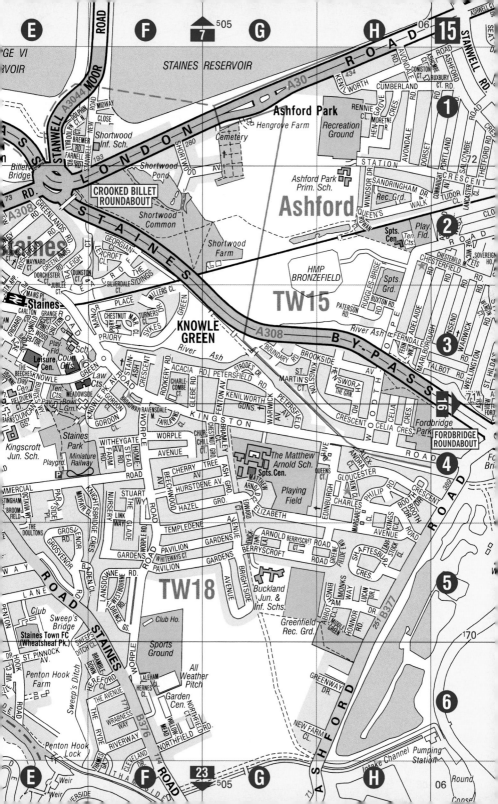

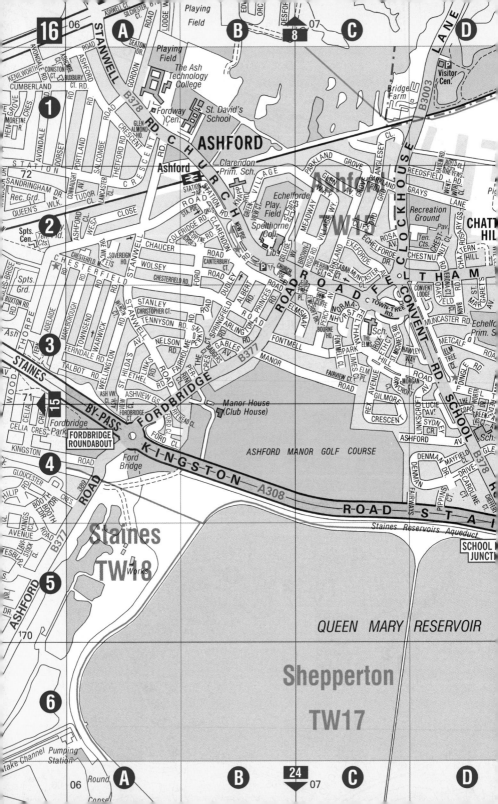

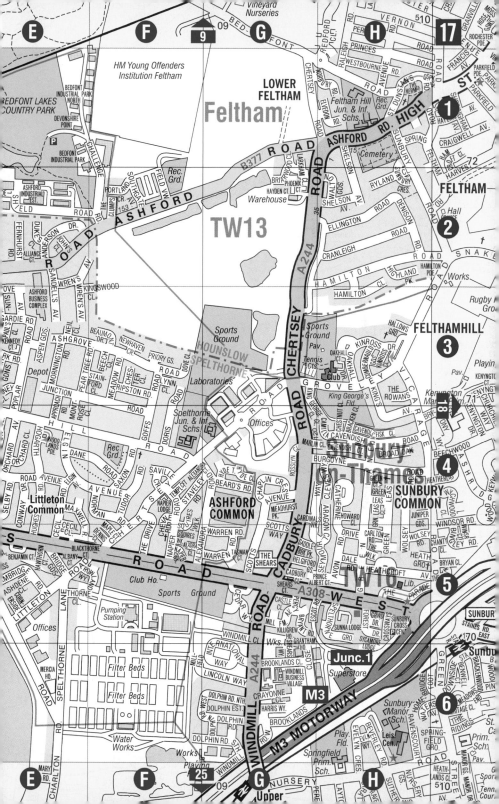

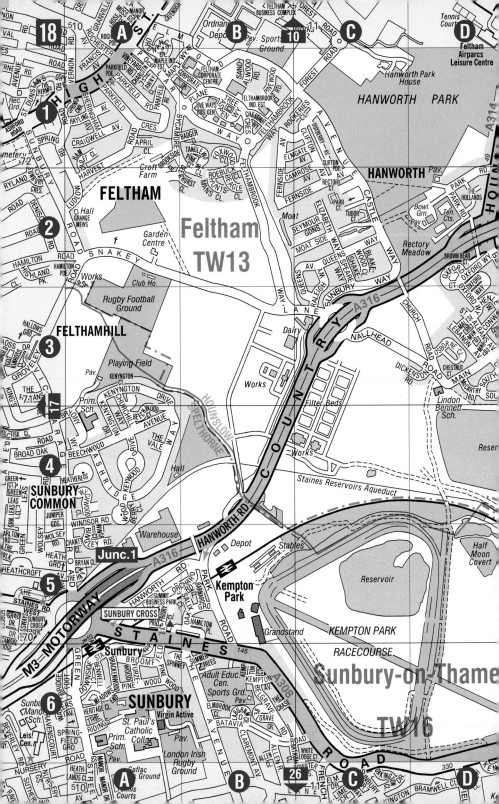

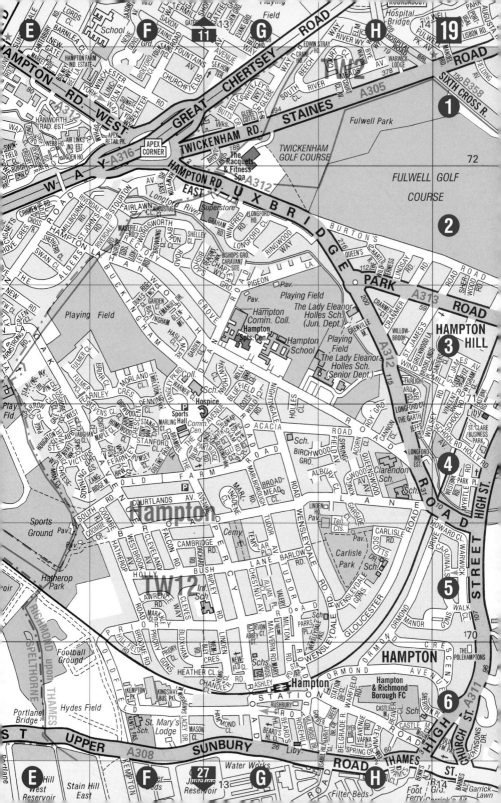

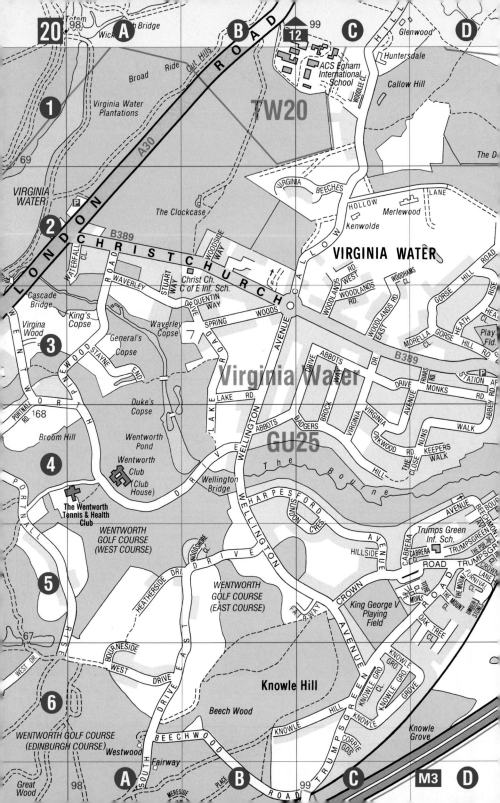

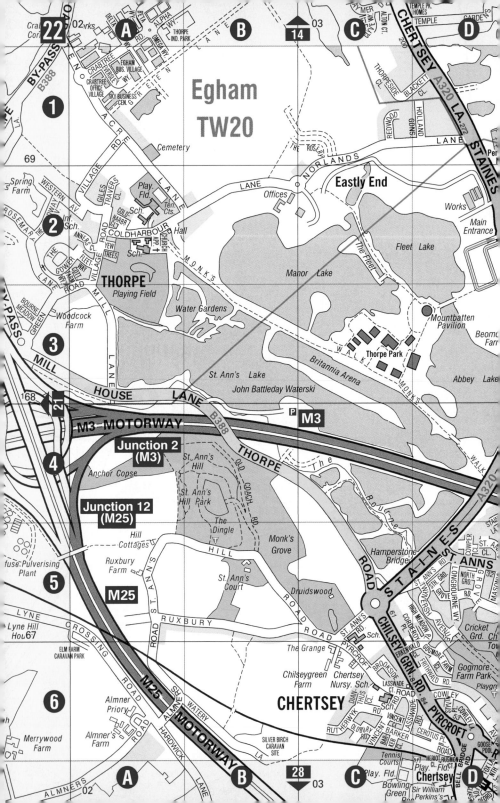

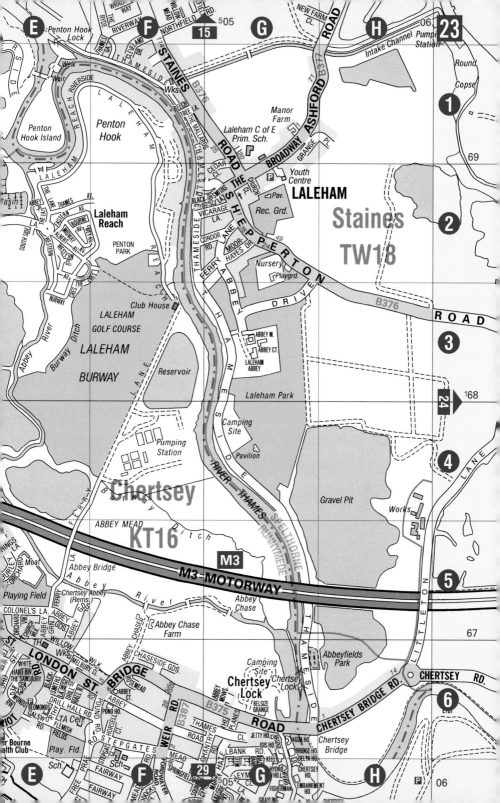

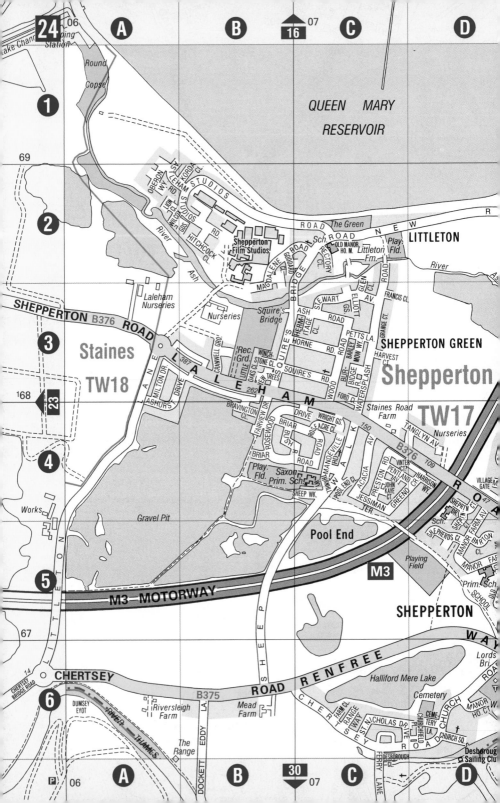

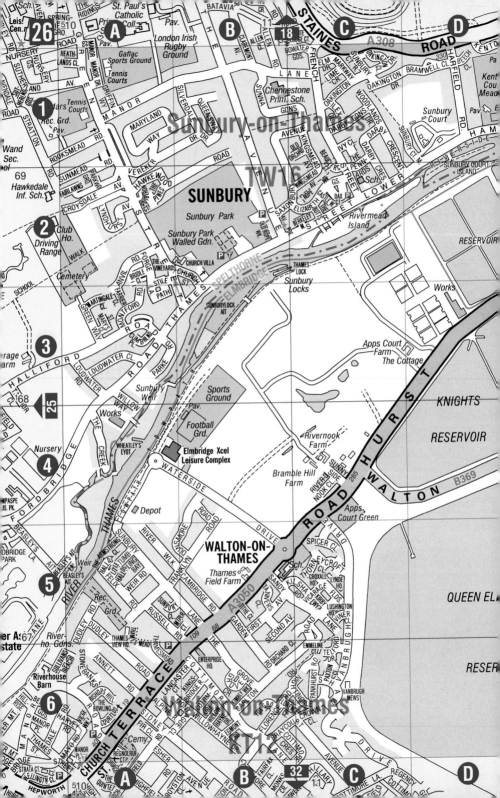

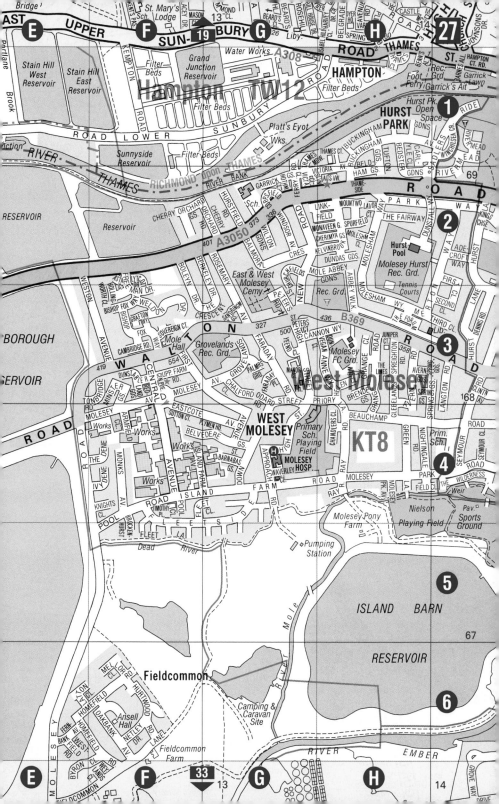

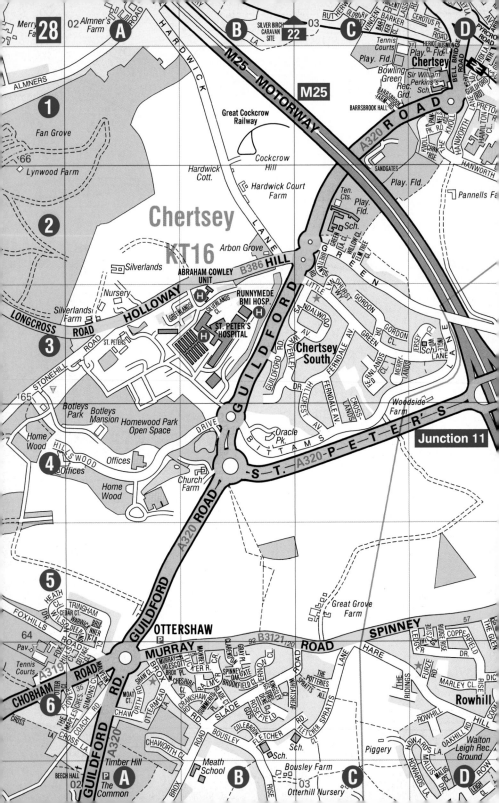

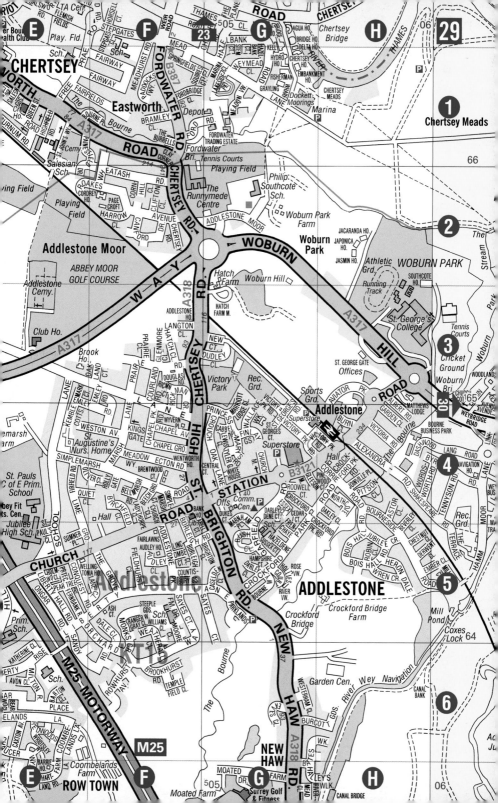

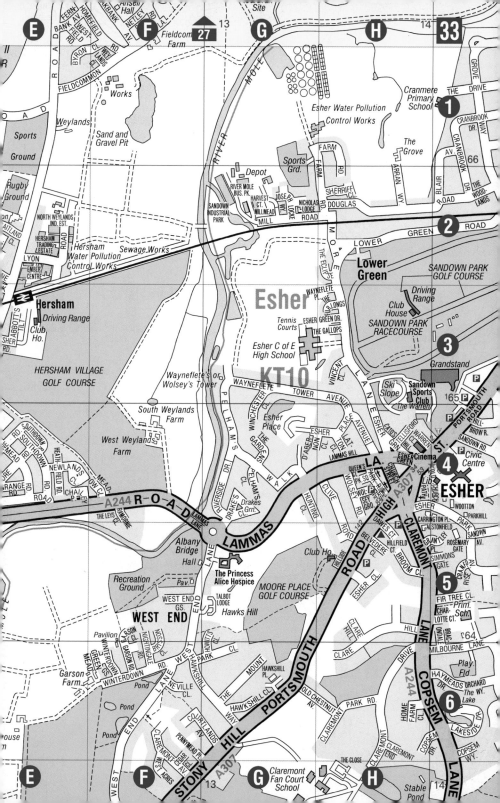

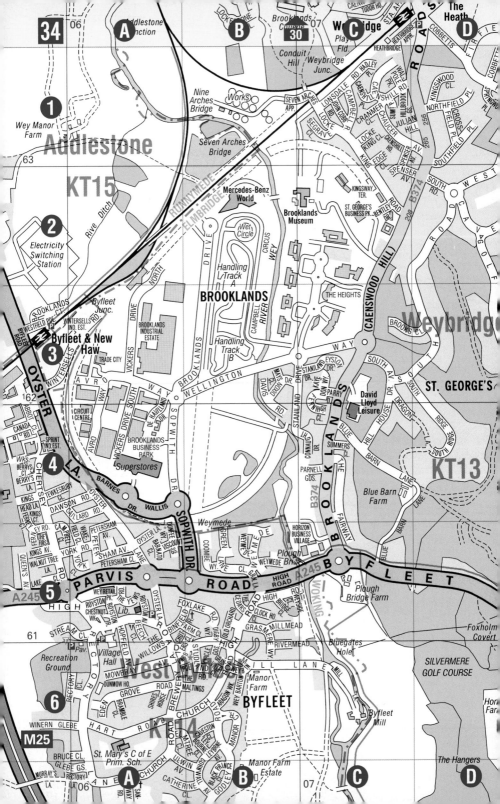

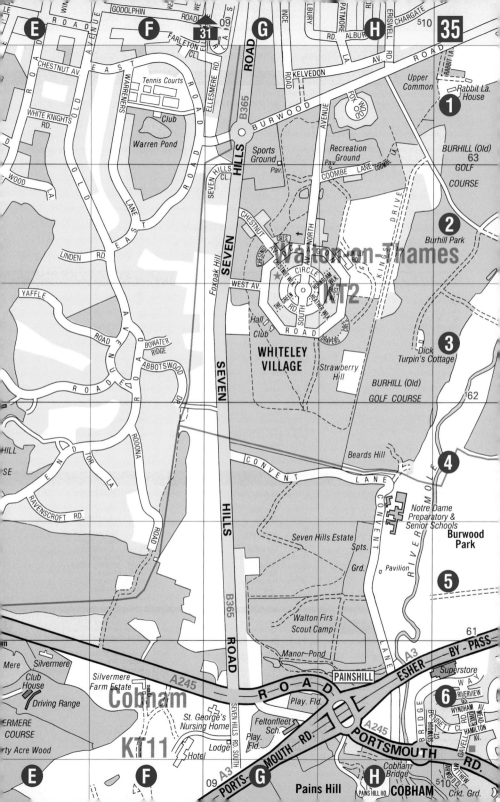

INDEX

Including Streets, Places & Areas, Hospitals & Hospices, Industrial Estates,
Selected Flats & Walkways, Junction Names, Stations, and Selected Places of Interest.

HOW TO USE THIS INDEX

1. Each street name is followed by its Postcode District, then by its Locality abbreviation(s) and then its map reference;
   e.g. **Abbey Dr.** TW18: Lale . . . .2G **23** is in the TW18 Postcode District and the Laleham Locality and is to be found in square 2G on page **23**. The page number is shown in bold type.

2. A strict alphabetical order is followed in which Av., Rd., St., etc. (though abbreviated) are read in full and as part of the street name;
   e.g. **Ash Ct.** appears after **Ashcombe Cl.** but before **Ashdale Cl.**

3. Streets and a selection of flats and walkways too small to be shown on the maps, appear in the index with the thoroughfare to which it is connected shown brackets; e.g. **Agnes Scott Cl.** KT13: Weyb . . . .3D **30** (off Palace Dr.)

4. Addresses that are in more than one part are referred to as not continuous.

5. Places and areas are shown in the index in BLUE TYPE and the map reference is to the actual map square in which the town centre or area is located and not to the place name shown on the map; e.g. ADDLESTONE 4G 29

6. An example of a selected place of interest is Brooklands Mus. 2B 34

7. An example of a station is Addlestone Station (Rail) . . . .4H 29. Included are Rail (Rail) and London Underground Stations (Tube)

8. Junction names are shown in the index in BOLD CAPITAL TYPE; e.g. APEX CORNER 1F 19

9. An example of a hospital is ASHFORD HOSPITAL 6A 8

GENERAL ABBREVIATIONS

All. : Alley	**Ga.** : Gate	**Pas.** : Passage
App. : Approach	**Gt.** : Great	**Pl.** : Place
Av. : Avenue	**Grn.** : Green	**Ri.** : Rise
Bri. : Bridge	**Gro.** : Grove	**Rd.** : Road
Bus. : Business	**Ho.** : House	**Rdbt.** : Roundabout
Cvn. : Caravan	**Ho's.** : Houses	**Shop.** : Shopping
Cen. : Centre	**Ind.** : Industrial	**Sth.** : South
Cir. : Circus	**Info.** : Information	**Sq.** : Square
Cl. : Close	**Junc.** : Junction	**Sta.** : Station
Coll. : College	**La.** : Lane	**St.** : Street
Comn. : Common	**Lit.** : Little	**Ter.** : Terrace
Cnr. : Corner	**Lwr.** : Lower	**Twr.** : Tower
Cotts. : Cottages	**Mnr.** : Manor	**Trad.** : Trading
Ct. : Court	**Mdw.** : Meadow	**Up.** : Upper
Cres. : Crescent	**Mdws.** : Meadows	**Vw.** : View
Cft. : Croft	**M.** : Mews	**Vs.** : Villas
Dr. : Drive	**Mt.** : Mount	**Vis.** : Visitors
E. : East	**Mus.** : Museum	**Wlk.** : Walk
Est. : Estate	**Nth.** : North	**W.** : West
Fld. : Field	**Pal.** : Palace	**Yd.** : Yard
Flds. : Fields	**Pde.** : Parade	
Gdns. : Gardens	**Pk.** : Park	

LOCALITY ABBREVIATIONS

Add : **Addlestone**	Hers : **Hersham**	Stan M : **Stanwell Moor**
Ashf : **Ashford**	Hort : **Horton**	Sun : **Sunbury**
Bedf : **Bedfont**	Houn : **Hounslow**	Thorpe : **Thorpe**
Byfl : **Byfleet**	Lale : **Laleham**	Twick : **Twickenham**
Chert : **Chertsey**	H'row A : **London Heathrow Airport**	Vir W : **Virginia Water**
Cobh : **Cobham**	Longc : **Longcross**	Walt T : **Walton-on-Thames**
E Mos : **East Molesey**	Lyne : **Lyne**	W Byf : **West Byfleet**
Egh : **Egham**	New H : **New Haw**	W Mole : **West Molesey**
Eng G : **Englefield Green**	Old Win : **Old Windsor**	Weyb : **Weybridge**
Esh : **Esher**	Ott : **Ottershaw**	W Vill : **Whiteley Village**
Felt : **Feltham**	Poyle : **Poyle**	Whitt : **Whitton**
Hamp : **Hampton**	Shep : **Shepperton**	Wind : **Windsor**
Ham H : **Hampton Hill**	Staines : **Staines**	Wray : **Wraysbury**
Hanw : **Hanworth**	Stanw : **Stanwell**	

A

Abbey Chase KT16: Chert 6F 23
Abbey Ct. KT16: Chert 6F 23
   TW12: Hamp 5G 19
   TW18: Lale 3G 23
Abbey Dr. TW18: Lale 2G 23
Abbey Fit Sports Cen. 4E 29
Abbey Gdns. KT16: Chert 5E 23
Abbey Grn. KT16: Chert 5E 23
Abbey Mdws.
   KT16: Chert 6G 23
Abbey M. TW18: Lale 3G 23
Abbey Pl. TW18: Staines 2E 23
Abbey Rd. GU25: Vir W 4D 20
   KT16: Chert 6F 23
   TW17: Shep 1C 30
Abbey Wlk. KT8: W Mole 2H 27

Abbot Cl. KT14: Byfl 4A 34
   TW18: Staines 5H 15
Abbots Dr. GU25: Vir W 4B 20
Abbots Way KT16: Chert 6D 22
Abbotswood KT13: Weyb 3H 31
Abbotswood Dr. KT13: Weyb 3F 35
Abbott Cl. TW12: Hamp 4E 19
Abbott's Tilt KT12: Hers 3E 33
Abell Cl. KT15: Add 5F 29
ABRAHAM COWLEY UNIT 3B 28
Acacia Av. KT17: Shep 4C 24
Acacia Rd. TW12: Hamp 4G 19
   TW18: Staines 3F 15
               (not continuous)
Acorn Cl. TW12: Hamp 4H 19
ADDLESTONE 4G 29
Addlestone Ho. KT15: Add 3F 29
ADDLESTONE MOOR 2E 29

Addlestone Moor KT15: Add 2G
Addlestone Pk. KT15: Add 5F
Addlestone Rd. KT13: Weyb 4A
   KT15: Add 4A
Addlestone Station (Rail) 4H
Adecroft Way KT8: W Mole 2H
Adelaide Pl. KT13: Weyb 4F
Adelaide Rd. KT12: Walt T 3A
   TW15: Ashf 3H
Admiral Stirling Ct.
   KT13: Weyb 3D
                    (off Palace)
Agnes Scott Cl. KT13: Weyb 3D
                    (off Palace)
Agua Ho. KT16: Chert 6G
Air Forces Memorial 2D
Air Links Ind. Est. TW13: Hanw 1E
Air Pk. Way TW13: Felt 6B
Airport Way TW19: Stan M 1
Aits Vw. KT8: W Mole 2H